RL 3.3
Pts 0.5
Quiz 75202

First Facts™

Materials

Metal

by Sara Louise Kras

Consultant:
Alan Russell
Associate Professor of Materials Science and Engineering
Iowa State University
Ames, Iowa

Capstone
press

Mankato, Minnesota

First Facts is published by Capstone Press
151 Good Counsel Drive, P.O. Box 669, Mankato, Minnesota 56002
www.capstonepress.com

Library of Congress Cataloging-in-Publication Data
Kras, Sara Louise.
    Metal / Sara Louise Kras.
    p. cm.—(First facts. Materials)
    Includes bibliographical references and index.
    Contents: Metal—What are metals?—Mining metals—Smelting metal—Mixing metals—Bend without breaking—Metal's many uses—Recycling metal—Amazing but true!—Hands on.
    ISBN 0-7368-2512-6 (hardcover)
    1. Metal—Juvenile literature. [1. Metals.] I. Title. II. Series.
TN667.K73 2004
669—dc22   2003015024

Credits
Heather Adamson and Blake A. Hoena, editors; Jennifer Bergstrom, series designer; Wanda
    Winch and Deirdre Barton, photo researchers; Gary Sundermeyer, photographer; Eric
    Kudalis, product planning editor

Photo Credits
Capstone Press/Gary Sundermeyer, cover, 1, 5, 6–7, 11, 16, 17, 19
Corbis/Adam Woolfitt, 10; Charles E. Rotkin, 9
Digital Vision, 14–15
Image Ideas Inc./Jacob Halaska, 12–13
Photodisc/PhotoLink/Annie Reynolds, 8

1 2 3 4 5 6 09 08 07 06 05 04

Table of Contents

Metal

Sandy waits next to the bus stop sign. She looks at her watch. Then she counts her coins. She has enough money for the bus fare and a can of soda. Sandy pulls up her coat zipper as the bus arrives. Metal objects are all around us.

What Are Metals?

Most metals are not natural products. People get materials for metals from **ores**. Ores are found in Earth's **crust**. Ores are rocks that contain materials needed to make metals. Metals can be formed into items people use every day.

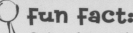 **Fun Fact:**
Only a few metals, such as gold and silver, are found in nature in their pure form.

Mining Metals

People mine metal ores to remove them from the ground. Some mining takes place near Earth's surface. Miners dig pits to get ore close to the surface.

Miners dig tunnels to reach metal
ores far underground. Miners go down
deep holes to find metals like lead.

9

Smelting Metal

Most metal ores must be **smelted** before they can be used. Smelting heats the ore and separates the metal from the rock. Pure metal is left behind.

Metal ores also can be smelted using chemicals and **electricity**. Aluminum is used to make soda cans. It comes from an ore that is smelted by electricity.

Mixing Metals

Mixing metals creates new kinds of metals. Metal mixtures are called **alloys**. Aluminum is a lightweight alloy that does not **rust**.

Metals also can be mixed with nonmetals. Adding carbon to iron makes steel. Steel is stronger than iron. It is used to build bridges.

14

E.T.C (R-598

Bend without Breaking

Metals are strong. Metals like steel and aluminum can be shaped into trains, ships, and airplanes. The shaped metal bends only slightly. It is strong enough to carry heavy loads without breaking.

Metal's Many Uses

Metals have many uses. Metals carry heat and electricity. Metal wires bring electricity to computers, TVs, and lights.

Stainless steel does not rust and is easy to clean. Most forks, knives, and spoons are made of stainless steel.

Recycling Metal

Metal does not have to be thrown away after it is used. Metal can be melted down and used again. **Recycled** steel becomes shiny new cars. Recycled aluminum is used to make new cans. Recycling helps make sure there will be plenty of metal for the future.

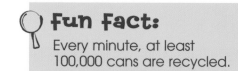

Fun Fact:
Every minute, at least 100,000 cans are recycled.

The planet Jupiter is a giant ball of metal. Jupiter's outer gas layer crushes hydrogen gas from the planet's center. The pressure turns the hydrogen into metal.

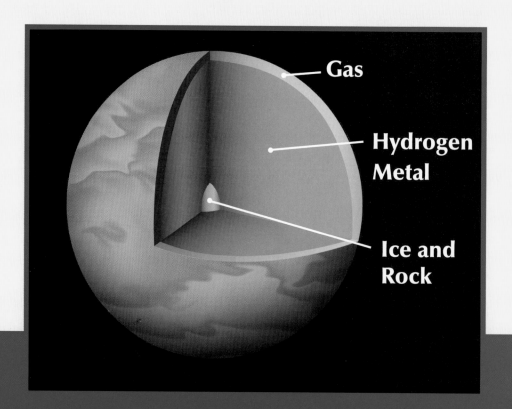

Gas

Hydrogen Metal

Ice and Rock

Hands On: Metal Conducts

Metals are conductors. Conductors carry heat and electricity better than other materials. Try this experiment to see if metal conducts heat better than wood or plastic.

What You Need

small container
hot water
metal spoon
plastic spoon
small wooden stick

What You Do

1. Fill the small container with hot water.
2. Stand the metal spoon, plastic spoon, and stick in the container so that one end of each object is in the water.
3. Wait a few minutes. Then feel the dry ends of the spoons and the stick. Which object feels the warmest? Which material conducts heat the best?

Cooking pots often have plastic or wooden handles because metals are conductors. If a pot's handle were metal, it would get too hot to hold.

Glossary

alloy (AL-oi)—a mixture of two or more metals

crust (KRUHST)—Earth's outer layer

electricity (ee-lek-TRISS-uh-tee)—a form of energy used to power lights and other machines

ore (OR)—a rock that contains metal

recycle (ree-SYE-kuhl)—to make used items into new products

rust (RUHST)—the forming of a reddish brown substance on iron and steel when they are exposed to water or air

smelt (SMELT)—to melt ore so that the metal can be removed from the rock

Read More

Baldwin, Carol. *Metals.* Material Matters. Chicago: Raintree Steck-Vaughn, 2004.

Mitchell, Melanie S. *Metal.* First Step Nonfiction. Minneapolis: Lerner, 2003.

Internet Sites

FactHound offers a safe, fun way to find Internet sites related to this book. All of the sites on FactHound have been researched by our staff.

Here's how:
1. Visit *www.facthound.com*
2. Type in this special code **0736825126** for age-appropriate sites. Or enter a search word related to this book for a more general search.
3. Click on the Fetch It button.

FactHound will fetch the best sites for you!

Index